Feasts of Feasts

Advent, Christmas, and Epiphany with St. Francis

The scripture quotations in this book of devotions are from The New Revised Standard Version Bible, copyright ©1989 by the Division of Christian Education of the National Council of the Churches of Christ in the U.S.A., and are used by permission. All rights reserved.

©2022 Episcopal Diocese of Georgia
All rights reserved

Cover Art

The front cover painting is a detail from Madonna and Child with Saints Francis and Jerome (c. 1512-1515) by Francesco Francia. The Child holds a pair of cherries, a reference to the sacrificial blood of Christ. To the Virgin's right is Saint Francis wearing the traditional tonsure and heavy monastic robes. In his 1568 edition of the Artist's Lives, the sixteenth-century biographer and painter Giorgio Vasari described Francia's "sweet harmony of coloring" that prompted people to run "like madmen to this new and more lifelike beauty." Vasari saw Francia as an artist at the verge of a new and exciting age of painting, which would be realized fully by Leonardo da Vinci, Raphael, and Michelangelo. This painting is one of 492,000 of works of art that The Met has placed in the public domain. It is part of the Robert Lehman Collection at The Met. All artwork in this book is courtesy of The Met. Photos are courtesy of the authors.

Feasts of Feasts

Advent, Christmas, and Epiphany with St. Francis

Frank & Victoria Logue

A study for a painting of Saint Francis Renouncing His Worldly Goods by Luigi Garzi (c. 1696)

Forward

"He was a poet whose whole life was a poem."

-G.K. Chesterton on Francis of Assisi

Francis of Assisi did not simply believe in Jesus as God's son as in agreeing to statements of faith. Francis believed so wholeheartedly, his faith transformed his life, embodying the Gospel in actions and not just words.

We see this way of living out Jesus' teachings when Francis' father, Pietro de Bernardone, brought his idealistic son before Bishop Guido II of Assisi. Francis had refused to obey his father, and had even sold some fine cloth and a horse his father had given him, using the proceeds to cover part of the cost of rebuilding the ruined San Damiano Chapel. After imprisoning him in his home for a time, his father ended up bringing him before the bishop. In that dramatic meeting, Francis renounced his father saying, "Before, I called you 'father,' but now I only have one

Father who is in heaven." Then living out the meaning of his proclamation, he removed all his clothes. Seeing that he had given away all his possessions, the bishop wrapped his mantle around Francis.

Francis was not alone in his family with a flare for the dramatic. There is a story of his mother, Pica, having a stable built so that she could give birth to her son there. This story is preserved in an old manuscript at the Vatican. It says as she began to feel labor pains, a stranger dressed as a pilgrim told Pica that the child would not be born until she was in a stable. Tradition has it this chapel dedicated to "St. Francis, the Little One," marks the stable she had built for the purpose. There in the "Stalleta," she gave birth to the boy she named Giovanni for John the Baptist. His father called him Francesco, meaning "French," from which we get Francis. In an echo from this story of his own birth, Francis had a manger built in a cave for the first live Nativity for the Christmas Mass, as a way of enacting Jesus' birth on the Feast of the Incarnation.

Francis elevated the season of Advent through Christmastide to Epiphany as he saw that God entering into creation in the person of Jesus was the central fact of human history. The Incarnation changed everything. God became human. The Holy Trinity would not stand back as a righteous judge, but entered into the creation to weave the tattered tapestry of creation back from the inside. So while he loved Easter—the Charity of the Passion, he called it—he proclaimed Christmas as the "Feast of Feasts." For in the Nativity, the Second Person of the Trinity became human.

Since at least the last half of the 6th century, the season of Advent has been set aside as a time of preparation for Jesus' Second Coming even as we prepare to celebrate God becoming human in Jesus. Advent is sometimes thought of as a little Lent, a time for self-examination and asking for forgiveness. With Christmas itself increasingly a holiday cut off from its purpose of celebrating the birth of Jesus Christ, reclaiming the season of Advent is all the more urgent.

This devotional will take you from Advent through the Epiphany. While we will share stories from the life of Francis and quotes from him and other Franciscans, these readings are intended to put our focus less on Francis and more how we might live the Gospel in our own lives through this season of preparation for Jesus' return in glory.

The goal of these weeks is to learn to follow Jesus more closely by seeing our savior in the example of Francis. For in living out the Gospel, Francis was merely replicating Jesus' method. Jesus did not just teach humility, but lived it by serving rather than being served. Jesus did not just teach us about godly compassion through the Parable of the Good Samaritan. Jesus enacted that compassion in every encounter. Likewise, Francis did not just speak of peace, as we will read in this devotional, he offered himself to the

Sultan who was fighting against Christians in the Holy Land.

To assist your journey through the season, we have organized the seven weeks of this devotional around some distinctively Franciscan ways of following Jesus: humility, simplicity, compassion, peace, love, creation, and joy. Each week, we will explore these themes through Franciscan stories, stories from our own lives, a prayer on the theme, and a Francisan quotation as well as reflections on service and worship viewed through that theme for the week. The hope is that we too might act on these virtues in our daily lives, and so not simply read about humility, but change our actions based on what we learn.

We are offering a video each week that develops the theme further. These are posted on the diocesan YouTube Channel at https://www.youtube.com/georgiaepiscopal

Advent I
Humility

Francis of Asissi longed to follow Jesus in a life grounded in profound humility. In the Second Person of the Holy Trinity becoming human, the Incarnation, Francis found this ideal of humility made complete, so that Christmas was the pinnacle of the church year. Thomas of Celano wrote that "Francis observed the birthday of the child Jesus with inexpressible eagerness over all other feasts."

We read of the humility that is at the heart of the Incarnation in Philippians (2:3-8), "Let the same mind be in you that was in Christ Jesus, who, though he was in the form of God, did not regard equality with God as something to be exploited, but emptied himself, taking the form of a slave, being born in human likeness. And being found in human form, he humbled himself and became obedient to the point of death— even death on a cross."

For Francis, if even God could humble himself in taking on humanity, how much more should we who follow Jesus do the same?

Sunday – A Franciscan Story

"Do nothing from selfish ambition or conceit, but in humility regard others as better than yourselves. Let each of you look not to your own interests, but to the interests of others."

-Philippians 2:3-4

Francis of Assisi was born into the age of chivalry when troubadours entranced their audiences with stories of heroic knights and the virtues of courtly love. These songs became deeply influential for Francis, the son of a wealthy textile merchant. His friend and early biographer, Bonaventure, would write that Francis was reared "in vanity amid the vain sons of men."

Francis saw an opportunity for the glory found in battle when, at 20, he and other young men from Assisi enlisted to fight against the neighboring Umbrian hill-town of Perugia. Assisi lost the battle. Francis was imprisoned for a time. Defeat in battle and the illness that followed in prison caused Francis to turn away from all notions of finding glory in combat.

Later, on a pilgrimage to Rome, Francis saw a beggar outside of St. Peter's Church. The Holy Spirit moved him to trade places with a beggar. Francis exchanged clothes with the man and then spent the day begging for alms. That experience of poverty shook Francis to the core. He would in time find his ideals of courtly love in the Blessed Virgin Mary and in Lady Poverty. In them, Francis saw the paradoxes of the Gospel—richness in poverty, life in death, strength in weakness.

Within his lifetime Francis would rise to a fame that would have pleased his younger self, but he was dismissive of his having accomplished anything. Outwardly, this was far from true. By the time of his death, Francis had accomplished much by any standard. Francis' followers became the Order of Friars Minor. The group was endorsed by the Church and a similar order was established for women, and yet a third for married persons who wanted to keep a rule of simplicity appropriate to them.

Francis could see the thousands of lives transformed by his call for deep repentance and radical simplicity of life. Francis' own example of a Christ-like life transformed the Italy of his youth within his own lifetime. Yet he continued to see himself rightly, not considering himself more than he should. This is why from his deathbed, Francis said to his fellow friars, "Let us begin, brothers, to serve the Lord our God for up to now we have made little or no progress."

Given the immensity of need in the world and the continued suffering of the poor, Francis saw how much more could be accomplished if followers of Jesus looked not just to their own interests, but also showed concern for others. Our journey through Advent to Christmas and beyond is not about beating ourselves up. Humility is found in right-sizing how we see ourselves. Once we get realistic about ourselves, we can make changes to become more Christ-like as we look not just to our own interests, but to those of others.

Monday – A Prayer

Almighty and eternal God, your Son our Savior Jesus Christ emptied himself to be born in human form and humbled himself and became obedient to the point of death, even death on a cross. Grant us the grace to see ourselves rightly and give to us the strength of purpose to so love our neighbors as ourselves that we look not to our own interests, but also to the interest of others. This we pray that the same mind may be in us that was in Christ Jesus, who lives and reigns with you and the Holy Spirit, one God, now and forever. *Amen.*

Advent, Christmas, and Epiphany with St. Francis

Tuesday – Victoria's Reflection

In our Lenten devotional, *A Spring in the Desert*, I wrote about confusing low self-esteem with humility. In the Principles that are a part of the rule for the Third Order, Society of Saint Francis, Day Twenty-four states: "Nevertheless, when asked to undertake work of which we feel unworthy or incapable, we do not shrink from it on the grounds of humility, but confidently attempt it through the power that is made perfect in weakness."

It is so easy to think you're being humble when you are, in fact, hiding your fear that you might not be capable of doing something.

But, before that, Day Twenty-Three notes: "Humility confesses that we have nothing that we have not received and admits the fact of our insufficiency and our dependence upon God. It is the basis of all Christian virtues. Saint Bernard of Clairvaux said, 'No spiritual house can stand for a moment except on the foundation of humility.' It is the first condition of a joyful life within any community." And that is whether the community is your own home, where you work, or your church.

I remember once that I put a lot of time and effort into putting on an event and was quite proud when I saw that it was going well. And yet, when it was over, someone else claimed the credit for its success. My first reaction was anger. "What am I? Chopped liver?" I thought. But, by this point, I had been a Franciscan for a number of years. I gritted my teeth, took a deep breath, and reflected instead. Would it change anything in a helpful way if I spoke up or let it be known that I had done most of the work? The answer was 'no'. No, it wouldn't. In fact, it would probably only embarrass the person receiving the accolades and cause a rift in our relationship.

So, I said nothing. And now, years later, I can no longer even remember the details of the event or who it was that allowed themselves to be congratulated on the work done. Sometimes humility is simply not saying anything.

St. Francis of Assisi Adoring the Christ Child by Claude Mellan.

Questions for reflection
Have you ever been given credit for something someone else has done? Or alternatively, not taken the credit when it should have been yours? How did you feel and what did you do about it?

Wednesday – Quotations

"You eat from the Tree of the Knowledge of Good when you appropriate to yourself your own will, thus crediting yourself with the good which the Lord says and does in you."

–*Saint Francis in the Admonition, 2*

Questions for reflection
Have you ever taken more credit for something than you should have?

And, as Francis notes, do you feel that the good things you have done are done by your will alone or do you give God credit for helping you to see that you are capable of goodness?

Thursday – Service

Humility is a right view of oneself, that is neither prideful nor self-abasement. This is true for all of what are called the seven deadly sins. There is a healthy mid-point that is the goal and the sin lies on either side of that moderation. For example, gluttony is usually thought of as the sin of eating too much, and it is. But, according to Saint Augustine's Prayer Book, gluttony can also be expressed in eating too little, such as in the eating disorder anorexia. A healthy appetite is good. Gorging on too much food or erring toward self-denial both fall short of the mark. In this same way, pride can be expressed in being all about yourself, taking up too much space, barging in on every conversation. But that same error is seen in holding back your gifts and failing to bring your whole self, with all the gifts God has given you.

Questions for reflection
As you consider the ways in which you serve others, using the gifts you have been given, are there ways in which you have been holding back?

In what way might you offer more of your unique gifts to bear in serving others?

Friday – Frank's Reflection

I suspect that humility is rarer than I care to admit among those elected and ordained as bishops. I certainly have bishop colleagues in whom I see no signs of vainglory. Yet, one does not trip and fall and find oneself in a bishop's election by accident. And the election process requires one to demonstrate some qualities that seem Episcopal. Without a bit of "look at me" on the part of a priest, our current process of selecting a chief pastor is unlikely to end up with the more self-effacing priest on the slate of nominees.

If you know me at all, you know that I am certainly chief among those who say, "Look at this thing I wrote!" or "Here is a photo I took!" So, I am not pretending to have nailed the humility that was central to the poor man of Assisi. But what I have noticed is that Jesus' teaching on humility is simply true, and we ignore it at our spiritual peril. He said, "All who exalt themselves will be humbled, and all who humble themselves will be exalted." This is how life works. When I get, in the parlance of my childhood, "too big for my britches," there is some humbling experience that will find me.

I was on the planning team for Evangelism Matters in 2016. The Rev. Alex Montes-Vela and I were asked to close out the gathering with a look back at the conference, naming what we had heard in the gathering. This meant that throughout the conference, we looked for the markers of the Holy Spirit where common threads wove through the meeting in presentations made by persons who did not know what the others would be saying. I did a little wrap-up with quotations from presenters, and Alex brought it home with a touching story that connected it all in a powerful way. The presentation seemed to work for the attendees. I was proud of what we had done. Not that there is anything wrong in feeling good about a job well done, but in retrospect, I was a little too impressed with myself. When asked to do the wrap-up for Evangelism Matters 2018, my part of the presentation was a little too cute, show-offy in a way not as subtle as I'd hoped. I hit the wrong notes right as the conference was concluding. Fortunately, the Rev. Canon Stephanie Spellers sensed this on the fly and course-corrected by saying more as she took the floor to offer a closing prayer and blessing that ended the meeting. Otherwise, we would have sent attendees out on a sour note. I knew I had messed up. And I knew the failure came out of being impressed with myself.

As I reflect on this, I see the many times I have let myself get a big head and, consequently, failed to prepare correctly or discern the right tone. At such times, my efforts have routinely fallen flat in ways that reflect on those who trusted me to bring my whole self, but not my whole prideful self. I have learned that I can get the presentation right, but only when I keep my pride in check and discern what God wants me to do or say.

Humility means bringing one's whole self, with all the gifts that you have, but doing so in a way that honors God.

Questions for reflection
Have you found yourself humbled when your ego takes center stage?

How have you held back from offering all the gifts you bring?

Saturday – Worship

"But whenever you pray, go into your room and shut the door and pray to your Father who is in secret, and your Father who sees in secret will reward you."

-Jesus in Matthew 6:6

Naturally, that doesn't mean we shouldn't worship in community, that is, go to church regularly. What it does mean, though, is that when we are in church, we should be careful not to bring undue attention to ourselves.

Cynthia Bourgeault, a modern-day mystic, Episcopal priest, writer, and internationally-acclaimed retreat leader, tells a story in her book, *Chanting the Psalms*, that is a good example of humility in worship.

She writes, "Everyone sings with a slightly different vocal instrument, and the beauty comes in blending them together through a subtle give-and-take. You also have to be aware of the space that the person next to you is taking up and avoid the temptation to wander off into a personal emotional high. I remember one evening at vespers with the monks at Saint Benedict's [monastery in Colorado] when I was so pleased that I knew a particular psalm tone well that I started singing with wonderful drama and verve, having myself a grand old time. Afterward, one of the monks pulled me aside and said very sweetly but pointedly, 'My choirmaster once told me, if you can't hear the person next to you, you're singing too loud.'"

Fortunately, Episcopal worship tends to be a very give-and-take style of worship, but it does offer opportunities to make a spectacle of oneself.

Question for reflection
Can you think of other ways in which to humble yourself in worship?

Advent II

Simplicity

"Take care! Be on your guard against all kinds of greed;
for one's life does not consist
in the abundance of possessions."

-Jesus in Luke 12:15

Jesus taught us to be careful where we store up treasure, whether on earth or in heaven, lest our possessions come to possess us. This does not mean one does not need the stuff of life, but that the better path is to remain detached in such a way that the things we own are not the most important part of our lives. And in simplifying our lives, we also find more time for a spiritual path. We see this in the life of Francis who embraced holy poverty and, in the process, was able to give so much to the people of his age from the spiritual wealth he accumulated.

Simplicity could be seen as a rigid rule, but we experience it more as a grace, a gift from God. We live in a 1925

The Bungalogue, our home in Savannah, Georgia.

bungalow in a less than prestigious part of Savannah. Our house reflects this Franciscan ideal for simplicity of life. Not that living in a 1,050-square foot house puts us on a path to holiness, but it does set limits on what we can acquire. The stuff we buy needs to fit this life. And the bins in the back of our two-car garage point to how much further we have to go in minimizing the stuff we own. Simplicity, no matter how we live into it, is the intentional way we focus our lives on what matters most to us.

Questions for reflection
Are there ways in which you would like your life to be more minimalistic? Where would you start?

Sunday – A Franciscan Story

Francis came of age in a family that was part of the new Italian middle class, an upward mobility unknown to previous generations. Italy in the 1200s, like much of the world at that time, was divided into the nobility and the rest. The nobles were the majors, *mayores* in Italian, and everyone else was *minores*, meaning minor. Francis' father, Pietro de Bernadone, moved his family from the minors to the majors through a thriving trade in textiles.

After Francis returned from his time as a prisoner of war, he was increasingly drawn to radically follow the Jesus he met in the Gospels. To chart his course, Francis looked to the Holy Spirit's guidance in finding inspiration from Jesus' life and ministry. One day, he went into the Church of Saint Nicholas in Assisi with his friend Bernard. The two opened a Gospel book three times, trusting that when they opened the pages and Francis put his finger on a random text, that the text under his finger would be a sign from God of how they should live.

Francis and Bernard had a child-like faith as they entered St. Nicholas Church. The Holy Spirit guided them to Matthew 19:21, which told them to "sell all that you have and give to the poor"; then to Luke 9:3, which said to "take nothing on the journey"; and then finally to Matthew 16:24, which said, "Follow me."

Those three passages were the signs the two needed to simplify their lives and focus on the poor. The example of first Francis and Bernard and then others dropping out of the up-and-coming set to simply follow Jesus was compelling. More and more young men joined the movement. In time, Francis founded a religious order, and he named it the Order of Friars Minor. Intentionally rejecting the *mayores*, the majors, Francis identified with the commoner, the lost, and the left out. He wanted for himself and those around him, a minor life, grounded in humility and trusting God. Clare of Assisi (1194-1253) later founded the Order of Poor Ladies. Francis then created a middle way for married men and women to follow Jesus as the monks and nuns did, while remaining married. He created a rule for this Franciscan Third Order, whose members are called tertiaries. All three orders emphasized simplicity as part of following Jesus in the way of Francis.

Monday – A Prayer

Most merciful God, your Son Jesus Christ looked with compassion on his friend Martha who was worried and distracted by her many tasks, teaching her there is need of only one thing, and extolling her sister Mary for choosing the better part. Assist us, we pray to do few things, and do them well, and to experience holiness in simple joys knowing that pure holy simplicity confounds all the wisdom of this world and the wisdom of the flesh. All this we ask in your holy Name. *Amen.*

Tuesday – Victoria's Reflection

The way of Saint Francis, who was inspired by Jesus, has been, since the beginning, open to whoever is free at heart from all material servitude. To live simply is the "Third Aim" of the Third Order.

As Days 10 through 12 read in our daily guiding principles: "The first Christians surrendered completely to our Lord and recklessly gave all that they had, offering the world a new vision of a society in which a fresh attitude was taken towards material possessions. This vision was renewed by Saint Francis when he chose Lady Poverty as his bride, desiring that all barriers set up by privilege based on wealth should be overcome by love. This is the inspiration for the third aim of the Society, to live simply.

"Although we possess property and earn money to support ourselves and our families, we show ourselves to be true followers of Christ and of Saint Francis by our readiness to live simply and to share with others. We recognize that some of our members may be called to a literal following of Saint Francis in a life of extreme simplicity. All of us, however, accept that we avoid luxury and waste, and regard our possessions as being held in trust for God.

"Personal spending is limited to what is necessary for our health and well-being and that of our dependents. We aim to stay free from all attachment to wealth, keeping ourselves constantly aware of the poverty in the world and its claim on us. We are concerned more for the generosity that gives all, rather than the value of poverty in itself. In this way we reflect in spirit the acceptance of Jesus' challenge to sell all, give to the poor, and follow him."

Because I read these principles monthly, simplicity of life is a constant undercurrent—what can I do to live my life more simply? This idea is very *au courant* right now. From Marie Kondo's *The Life-changing Magic of Tidying Up* to Swedish death cleaning, many people are looking for ways to simplify their lives and declutter their homes.

To be completely honest, I didn't begin the process of simplifying my life nearly 20 years ago when I became a postulant in the Third Order. Years earlier, Frank and I decided to start simplifying our lives after hiking the Appalachian Trail in 1988. It was that thru-hike that brought together my love of the outdoors and my love of simplicity (you can only carry so much in a backpack), and made me realize that Franciscan spirituality is my spiritual path.

So, with more than 30 years of simplifying under my belt, my advice would be to start slowly. Even 30-plus years later, I still have trouble letting go of books and plants! There are so many ways to simplify one's life—from material possessions to use of time. And there are many excellent resources out there to help you, from books and digital publications like *Simplify Magazine*, that can be found at: simplifymagazine.com

Wednesday – Quotations

"Whoever, then, would come to you [Lady Poverty], must ask you for it, and must enter it through you, for no one can enter the kingdom without the imprint of your seal."
—*Saint Francis in the Sacrum Commercium, 2-21*

The Bishop of Assisi once said to St. Francis, "I think your life is too hard, too rough. You don't possess anything in the world."

And Saint Francis replied, "My Lord, if we had possessions, we would need weapons to defend them."
—*The Anonymous of Perugia, Chapter III, 17*

Questions for reflection
How tied are you to your possessions?

Do you have a possession (an object not an animal or human) that you care for so deeply that you would use a weapon to defend it?

Thursday – Service

It is not uncommon to associate simplicity with poverty, but they are not the same thing. Simplicity is simply living close enough to the limits of our resources (not over) that we are able to rely on the love of God and appreciate the many wonders of God's creation.

In addition to simplifying our needs and possessions, the spirit of simplicity can be brought to bear on our relationships with other people as well as with God.

Questions for reflection
We often show our affection for other people with material gifts. Can you think of another way to practice simplicity toward those you care for that doesn't involve purchasing something?

And other than attending church and tithing, which should go without saying, can you think of other ways to offer yourself to God?

Advent, Christmas, and Epiphany with St. Francis

Friday – Frank's Reflection

On our wedding day in 1985, I was 22 years old. Victoria was 24. I find our ages startling in retrospect as I considered, at the time, that we waited to get married. My parents' marriage to one another was a second for each of them, and they were each in their teens when they were married for the first time. Victoria and I had been a couple for three years. We were out of college for 15 months by the day we exchanged our vows at St. George's Episcopal Church in Griffin, Georgia. We had been working together at the *Warner Robins Daily Sun* newspaper for most of that time, me as a photographer and Victoria as a writer.

Feast of Feasts

We were married well before Pinterest and other social media added more pressure for perfection, seeming to make weddings more performative. Our plan was to keep it simple. The goal was the sacrament of marriage. Victoria chose the wedding dress her mother, Laura Kelly, had worn 25 years earlier for her ceremony in the Chapel at the US Naval Academy. The dress had been handmade by Mary Griffin Kramp, Laura's grandmother, for her own wedding. Victoria and I worked with her family to make the food for the reception other than the bride and groom cakes. The groom's cake was a birthday cake for my mother's mother, Elizabeth Milligan Sullivan, whose 84th birthday fell on our wedding day. Victoria's stepmother, Deborah, made the bridesmaids' dresses and the outfit for our flower girl, Victoria's youngest sister, Kate.

I worked with my family to make all the flowers for the occasion. This was fitting as my Mom owned McGillis Flower Shop in Smyrna, Georgia. My brother, Michael, was an excellent designer working full-time as a florist as well. We mapped out our hopes for more naturalistic flowers and my Mom and brother went to a wholesale house in Atlanta charged with finding what looked good that day. Then that night after the rehearsal dinner, we gathered in a hotel room to put together everything we needed with the real pros handling the difficult pieces and most everyone taking part in assembling the bouquets, corsages, boutonnieres, and altar flowers.

I see value in the simplicity of those wedding plans. Most everything was made by our families with an emphasis, as with the flowers, on what was in season. This same path toward simple, fresh, and local has transformed cooking in our lifetimes, with top chefs taking the same attitude toward ingredients that my Mom and brother took toward the flowers for our wedding. What is in season? What looks good today? In this way we fit ourselves to the creation rather than bending the world to our desires.

I see in this the Franciscan desire for simplicity that goes with the flow, trusting that God is the source of the currents we ride. When we look for what is in season and fresh, we are going with rather than against creation. My mother's mother, whom we all called Gran, had always cooked this way. When she came to visit, we would invariably opt for the produce stand by the road. The corn looked good, and so we would eat corn on the cob one evening, and she would cut the corn the next day to make creamed corn. We might want the collards, but if they did not look good and the string beans did, then we would be snapping beans that afternoon.

Questions for reflection
What does simplicity look like in your life?

How might you opt for what is in season? What does fresh and local look like in aspects of your life far removed from cooking?

Saturday – Worship

In July and August of 2022, we experienced transcendent worship at Canterbury Cathedral while gathered with bishops and spouses from around the world for the Lambeth Conference of Anglican bishops. The liturgies offered the best of our tradition to the glory of God. We love the way physical spaces of great cathedrals embody both grandeur and mystery. They take one's breath away by their scale and have innumerable details that can be enjoyed, with the sense that there is always more to discover under the vaulted ceiling. The sounds of more than 1,100 bishops and spouses singing was exquisite. On the penultimate verse, the organ music fell away as the immense space filled with the sounds of praise formed from the accents of more than 165 countries singing in harmony.

The architectural wonder of an ancient cathedral filled with praise can take nothing away from the simple beauty of the Chapel of Our Savior along Honey Creek on the Georgia coast. There, surrounded by glass, the natural world of the salt marsh is one with simple wood lines of the ceiling. In the right light, the fingerprints of the builders captured in the varnish on the boards are visible. Simply beautiful. And when that chapel is filled with the voices of those gathered for a Happening or Cursillo closing service, nothing can match the joy.

Advent, Christmas, and Epiphany with St. Francis

Then there is the worship with no church walls at all, on the dock at Lake Blackshear with Christ Church, Cordele's Worship on the Water as the congregation arrives by boat each summer. Or compline on the beach at Tybee Island offered by All Saints' Church.

The people gathered in boats for Worship on the Water at the Resort Dock on Lake Blackshear.

And yet still, there is the worship of the Community of Saint Joseph, our ministry with persons who are homeless in Savannah. In a field with tents nearby in the woods, the congregation arrives on foot and by bike. The music there is offered by a group that blends those who slept in their own homes the night before playing and singing with those who spent the night nearby in a tent. This is not only worship for persons who are homeless, but with others who are living on the margins, as well.

While the setting could not be more different, the same ability for worship to be transformative is as present in the field church as it is in Canterbury Cathedral. There is nothing wrong and something quite wonderful with worshiping in grandeur, yet when all is stripped away to the essentials, Christ's presence in the bread and wine so transcends the setting as to be all the more meaningful. The Jesus whose second coming we await has already come in a cave used for a stable.

Questions for reflection
Reduced to the strictly necessary, what is essential in worship?

How might this inform or change all of our worship?

Advent III

Compassion

Compassion means feeling another person's pain and wanting to do something in order to relieve their suffering. The word *compassion*, itself, comes from Latin and means: to suffer together.

An excellent example of living with compassion in this day and age is Episcopal priest Becca Stevens, founder of Thistle Farms, an enterprise run by survivors of sexual abuse, trafficking, and addiction.

Stevens says: "My mother's example of showing love through practical means gave me the wherewithal to open a home for women survivors of trafficking, prostitution, and addiction more than twenty-five years ago in Nashville, Tennessee. It was a small house for five women. I said: 'Come live free for two years with no authority living with you....' I figured that's what I would want if I were coming in off the streets or out of prison....I did it because sanctuary is the most practical ideal of all.

"I wanted to do the work of healing from the inside out. And that begins with a safe home.

"From its humble beginning, Thistle Farms now has thirty global partners that employ more than 1,600 women. The mission to be a global movement for women's freedom is broad and is growing exponentially."

Stevens noted that in the beginning, it seemed silly to think that by starting a small community, they could somehow change the world. By the time Thistle Farms became a global movement, she realized that it was even sillier to believe that the world could change if all of us do nothing.

As Mother Teresa said, "Small things done with great love will change the world."

"There is no secret formula to experiencing the sacred in our lives," Stevens said. "It just takes practice and practicality. The deep truth of our lives and the fullness we are striving for don't happen with someone giving us the code to deep knowledge. Meaning and faith are not secret things. Sometimes what we need most is to remind one another of how the divine is all around us, calling us to see and taste it for ourselves."

Sunday – A Franciscan Story

Stories of the compassion of Saint Francis abound and it is difficult to choose just one. The saint was so deeply touched by the compassion of God that he wanted to show that same compassion to the world. Once fearful of lepers, he moved to the outskirts of Assisi to live with the lepers. It was there that he learned to see the lepers, and God, in a new way. He found loving compassion for the unlovable, the ugly, the despised. He began to understand the power of the saving love of God in the weakness of humanity.

One of the many examples of Francis' compassion occurred when he was at Colle in the province of Perugia. There he met a poor man whom he had known when he was still a young man with dreams of being a knight. He asked the man how he was faring. The man replied that his lord had taken everything he owned. As the poor man continued to curse the man who had robbed him of everything, Francis felt himself filled with pity for his former friend's soul.

"Brother, forgive your lord for the love of God," Francis told him, "so you may set your soul free, and it may be that he will return to you that which he has taken. Otherwise, you will lose not only your property but also your soul!"

His friend replied, "I cannot completely forgive him until he gives me back what he took."

Saint Francis removed his mantle and handed it to his friend. "Here, I'll give you this cloak," he said, "and beg you to forgive your lord for the love of God."

The man was so touched by the kindness of Francis that he took the gift and forgave the wrongs of his lord. Saint Francis learned to see the face of Jesus in each human he encountered. It did not matter if they were weak, sick, angry, greedy, or even hateful, he never judged or criticized others.

Questions for reflection
Can you think of a time in your own life when you were changed by an act of compassion from another person?

Can you think of someone who might be changed by a compassionate gesture from you?

Monday – A Prayer

Creator God, you hate nothing you have made, so that while we were yet sinners, you sent our Savior Jesus Christ to live among us. Looking with compassion on the crowds, seeing the harassed and helpless as being like sheep without a shepherd, he showed us how you are always seeking and saving the one that is lost. Give us the grace to suffer with those who suffer and to share the joy of those who rejoice as we love others with the love you have for us. This we ask for your mercy's sake. *Amen.*

Tuesday – Victoria's Reflection

Interesting word, *compassion*. It can embody anything from a friendly word and smile to going way out of your way on someone's behalf—helping a distressed motorist change a tire, mowing the yard for an elderly neighbor, visiting a sick friend in the hospital.

While we were thru-hiking the Appalachian Trail, we were the recipients of acts of compassion over and over again. We called it "Trail Magic", but it was really acts of kindness, compassion for two young backpackers. From complete strangers to former thru-hikers, we were continually shown compassion during our six-month hike.

One incident really sticks out because we remain in touch with the widowed wife of the couple to this day:

It was May of 1988, and we were hiking along the Blue Ridge Parkway in Virginia. That morning we were stopped by a Trail maintainer who kept us talking until a car pulled up. It was Bill and Laurie, the couple known by their trail name "The Happy Feet."

"Are you the Hawk and the Dove?" they asked, using our trail names. We replied in the positive, and they asked us where Craig, known as "The Estimated Prophet" was, and we said that he was a few minutes behind us. (It is common for former thru-hikers who live near the Trail to read the registers at Trail Shelters, so they know who is hiking that year.)

Craig showed up just about then, and they took us to Jellystone Park and bought us a 6-pack of beer and Snickers bars. Then they brought us back to the Trail, apologizing because they couldn't put us up for the night although we had not expected them to do so; the beer and candy were a welcome gift.

We started onwards again, and as we were approaching Cornelius Creek Shelter, we saw a piece of paper in the middle of the Trail. It was from the Happy Feet. The note said they'd pick us up at Petites Gap at 5:30 pm. It was already almost 3 pm, and the Gap was 9.5 miles away! It only took us a second to realize we wouldn't make it.

But Bill had left us an option! We could also hike to the Thunder Ridge Overlook that was six miles away. We left a note for Craig to tell him what we were doing and took off. We hiked hard but backpacking just takes longer and we realized that we weren't going to make it there, either.

Plan C. We hit the Forest Service Road at Parkers Gap and walked up to the Parkway. We hoped to get a ride there to Petites Gap. We left Craig a note at the junction of the road and trail telling him what we were planning on doing.

At the Overlook, we said hello to the man and woman seated there. The woman, Sandra, was also a Trail maintainer. I told her about meeting the Happy Feet, and our dilemma.

She said she'd take us to Petites Gap. Once there, we thanked her profusely and set down our packs. We had about an hour to wait. We were just finishing off our beers, and remarking that if Craig were smart, he'd do the same thing we'd done, when he arrived chauffeured by a congressman—the man we'd met with Sandra.

The hour flew by, and Bill arrived a bit early. It wasn't long before we were in Lynchburg and were shown to our sleeping space in the basement and handed towels for the shower on the second floor of their home.

Afterwards, feeling clean despite our dirty clothes, I rested on the sofa while Frank and Craig went to help Bill set up a zipline. When the party guests arrived, we joined them, and most of us took turns on the zipline.

Then it was dinnertime—chips, guacamole, cheese dip, burritos, and fajitas. After a while, the three of us headed back downstairs to see the slides from the Happy Feet's 1987 thru-hike. Frank and I played pool, watched an old movie briefly, talked a bit to Laurie and Bill, and soon headed to bed. We were even allowed to wash our clothes!

The next morning, we were treated to pancakes with apples and sausage. Stuffed, we said our farewells and were ferried back to the trail by Bill.

That was one of the most extravagant acts of compassion we experienced along the trail. We were also, at one point, given a free place to stay and treated like family, when Frank was recovering from shin splints. Tales of how often we were treated with compassion while backpacking could fill a book.

Questions for reflection
Have you been able to offer an act of compassion like this one? What was changed by the care you demonstrated?

Wednesday – Quotations

"The knowledge that changes the heart changes you and your interaction with the world, and that new way of knowing and acting changes the world around you and beyond you in space and time."

-Murray Bodo, Order of Friars Minor (OFM)

According to Herman Schaluck, OFM, there are four things we need in order to be fully compassionate: 1) contemplative seeing; 2) affective response; 3) practical help; and 4) sustained assistance.

Feeling empathy for someone or seeing a need somewhere is easily done as the world abounds with the poor and the needy, and there are so many wonderful causes that sometimes it is difficult to pick just one. The next steps are more difficult.

Questions for reflection
Have you ever seen a need and responded to it with practical help? What about with sustained assistance?

Thursday – Service

In July of 1977, Jean Donovan traveled to El Salvador where she worked as a lay missioner in La Libertad, along with Ursuline nun Dorothy Kazel. Working in the parish of the Church of the Immaculate Conception, they provided help to refugees of the Salvadoran Civil War and the poor, including shelter, food, transportation to medical care, as well as burying the bodies of the dead left behind by the death squads.

In the weeks before she was raped, tortured, and murdered by the death squads, Donovan wrote a friend, "Several times I have decided to leave El Salvador. I almost could, except for the children, the poor, bruised victims of this insanity. Who would care for them? Whose heart could be so staunch as to favor the reasonable thing in a sea of their tears and loneliness? Not mine, dear friend, not mine."

Shortly before she died, she said, "You can … make a big difference in the world if you realize that the world you are talking about might be very small—maybe one person, or two people. … If you can find a place to serve, you can be happy." I think Saint Francis would heartily agree.

Questions for reflection
Can you think of any instances when you have made a big difference in the world—even if that world consisted of only a person or two?

Are there ways you can continue to serve and make a big difference, or even a small difference with great love?

Friday – Frank's Reflection

Compassion is empathy in action, and as I reflect on this Christian virtue, I see that the Scoutmaster of my Boy Scout troop embodied this Christ-like response. Scouting was an important part of my childhood. I started out in Cub Scouts by attending my brother's meetings with my mom as the Den Mother. When I was finally old enough to be a Cub Scout, I joined Scouting and remained active all through elementary school, junior high, high school and my first year of college. Scouting was good to me. I got to see the world—twice backpacking out west at the Philmont Scout Ranch in New Mexico and traveling to England and

Sweden for the World Jamboree. But most importantly, I was in a troop that considered itself to be a ministry. The leaders were passing along the grace and love they received in Jesus.

My Scoutmaster was Gene McCord. At 6 foot 3, Mr. McCord was imposing for a young Scout. Mr. McCord was at times a rigid taskmaster as he expected your best from you. But over time, I came to see how Mr. McCord loved us fiercely. When I was 16, I had a couple of incidents Mr. McCord found out about. One time, I was driving a car while a buddy of mine from Scouts was throwing bottles at signs and mailboxes, just to hear them smash. Another time, I got mad at another friend, dropping him off at an unreasonable distance from home in a day long before cell phones. No one but me and God and those friends knew about these incidents. I know for a fact that the two friends would not have told Mr. McCord.

In each case, small town life was the tattletale. I was seen, and someone reported it back to Mr. McCord. He pulled me aside at a meeting and told me that I was not that kind of boy and would not be that kind of man. Mr. McCord made it clear that I would not continue down the new path I was on. There were no threats. There were no ultimatums. I had no choice but to stay on the straight and narrow path. Otherwise, he would know and I did not want to disappoint him.

Roughly twenty years later, I was asked to speak at a dinner given for Mr. McCord's retirement as a Scoutmaster after decades of service. I looked around at all my fellow Scouts from years before. I recounted this story, and then I said, "How can we possibly thank Gene McCord for all he did for us." The answer was clear. Paying him back is not possible or even the right idea. The way to thank Mr. McCord is to put our empathy into action for another generation. We had been shown compassion as Mr. McCord knew how tough the world was on teens. No one gets out of adolescence without significant bumps in the road. He and the other leaders had always connected their leadership in Scouting to faith in Jesus Christ. They wanted to be there for us in those formative years and their compassionate leadership made a critical difference.

Questions for reflection
Who has loved you at a time when you felt unlovable?

How might you be called to bring compassion to your relationships?

Saturday – Worship

Asking people how they came to faith in Jesus and then how they found the Episcopal Church is something I (Frank) love to do. One woman said she went by herself to church when she was 12. She was raised in New York City by parents who were not religious. One Sunday, she walked to the closest church, which was an Episcopal Church. A woman who she had learned to call a "bag lady" shuffled in with all her possessions after the service was well underway. She said she knew what was coming and she did not want to see the woman pushed back out onto the street. But that was not what occurred. The woman sat down in a pew behind a well-dressed woman wearing pearls, with every hair on her head in perfect place. She turned to face the bag lady and her face lit up! She smiled and moved to sit beside her as if she were an old friend she hadn't seen in years. The well-heeled woman opened her prayer book and went through the liturgy with the person who was homeless. She told me that she had no idea what the preacher said that Sunday. "I was hooked from that moment on," she told me. "It was absolutely compelling. I felt like I had seen Jesus in church that morning."

Questions for reflection
How might your welcome to others in worship show Christ-like compassion?

Feast of Feasts

What might you do differently on Sunday with this story in mind?

The Christus Rex in the Chapel of Our Savior at Honey Creek.

Advent IV

Peace

Peace is a complex term in the Franciscan sense. Francis understood peace more in the Hebrew sense of *Shalom*. But shalom implies more than lack of conflict. Shalom means completeness, soundness, welfare, and peace. It can also be translated as "success," and is used in that way as part of a blessing in 1 Chronicles 12:18. In its most straightforward sense, shalom refers to an external peace between two entities—such as individuals or nations—and to an internal sense of peace within the individual.

God's peace does not come to us easily. It is the kind of peace that lasts and was shown to us in the life of Jesus—His ministry, death, and resurrection. The entire aim of the ministry of Jesus was to establish a community so convinced they were beloved of God, they couldn't help but proclaim to others that they were beloved as well.

As former Third Order Franciscan, Archbishop Desmond

Tutu, said, "Do your little bit of good where you are; it's those little bits of good put together that overwhelm the world."

And in doing your "little bits of good" on a regular basis, you will not only grow more peaceful within, but the world, itself, will also become a little bit more peaceful.

Sunday – A Franciscan Story

To the medieval way of thinking, Muslims were "unbelieving profaners of the Holy Places." Even the popes at the time called them "enemies of the Cross of Christ," "dogs," "the most wicked lot of warriors," "a wicked people," and worse. And it was these popes along with bishops that inflamed the zeal of Christians to take part in Crusades to defeat this enemy.

This way of thinking was unfathomable to Saint Francis who saw in the Muslims he met not merely an opportunity for evangelism. He knew them as brothers, redeemed by the Blood of Jesus, and called to share in God's Kingdom. More importantly, he considered warfare diametrically opposed to the teachings of Jesus, who had treated humans with love and saved them by giving himself on the Cross.

So, Francis set out for the Crusades and the siege of Damietta, an Egyptian port city on the Mediterranean Sea into which the Nile flows. There, Sultan Melek el-Kamil was encamped across the Nile. Francis arranged to meet with him. As a chronicler at the time wrote:

"The Sultan not only dismissed Francis in peace, with wonder and admiration for the man's unusual qualities, but also received him fully into his favor, gave him a self-conduct by which he might go and come, with full permission to preach to his subjects, and an entreaty that he would frequently return to visit him."

Francis learned that a peaceful, humble, and courageous affirmation of the Christian faith—without causing offense to the conscience of the Muslims—could be respectfully heard in Muslim circles. And, while he was able neither to convert them nor to give his life as a martyr in so trying, he yet returned to Italy having won their respect.

Questions for reflection
Have you ever used a peaceful demeanor to ward off a potentially bellicose situation? How did the person or persons react when you refused to get angry?

How about a time, in hindsight, that using kind words and refusing to get ruffled would have produced a better result?

Monday – A Prayer

Eternal God, as our Savior Jesus spoke a word of peace to calm a storm, so give us that peace that the world can not give that while we are proclaiming peace with our lips, we might have it even more fully in our hearts. Assist us as we work toward peace among people and nations, that all might come within your most gracious reign. This we ask in the name of the King of Glory, the King of Peace, who lives and reigns with you and the Holy Spirit, one God for ever and ever. *Amen.*

Tuesday – Victoria's Reflection

Ever since I was a little girl I've aspired to a sense of inner peace and calm. Perhaps it was because my father could get violent when he was drunk. It didn't happen all the time, but when it did, it was memorable and none of us were spared his fury.

But to temper that, among the things my mother would do is read us *The Cherry Tree Carol* during Advent. I loved the story and how calm Mary stayed in the face of Joseph's jealousy and anger:

> Joseph and Mary walked
> Through an orchard green,

Where was cherries and berries
As thick as might be seen.

O then bespoke Mary,
So meek and so mild,
"Pluck me one cherry, Joseph,
For I am with child."

O then bespoke Joseph,
With words most unkind,
"Let him pluck thee a cherry
Who is father to thy child."

Mary looked at Joseph
And Mary hung her head,
"All I wanted, Joseph,
Is one cherry red."

We also had a stone statue of Mary in a little wooden triptych which I loved. There was something about unhooking the doors and opening them to reveal inside the little statue of Mary standing in her niche. The scent of the stone and old wood remains with me to this day. And, of course, I saw many paintings of Mary as I was growing up. It was the sense of calm and acceptance that Mary projected that I wanted to embody.

In the Principles of the Third Order, Day Twenty-Eight – The Third Note: Joy says at one point, "We carry within us an inner peace and happiness which others may perceive, even if they do not know its source." This is one of the many reasons the Third Order of Saint Francis appeals to me.

Yet, inner peace is not easily acquired. It is a long journey, a continual process of letting go—of letting go of anger, of hatred, of anxiety, of unforgiveness, of jealousy, of guilt, of shame…the list goes on, depending on what one needs to shed.

The fact is true peace begins within each of us. And each one of us has made the commitment in our Baptismal vows to: "strive for justice and peace among all people, and respect the dignity of every human being."

But, as Paul said in Philippians 4:6-7, "Do not worry about anything, but in everything by prayer and supplication with thanksgiving let your requests be made known to God. And the peace of God, which surpasses all understanding, will guard your hearts and your minds in Christ Jesus."

Advent, Christmas, and Epiphany with St. Francis

Wednesday – Quotation

Lord make us instruments of your peace.
Help us to recognize the evil latent in a communication that does not build communion.
Help us to remove the venom from our judgments.
Help us to speak about others as our brothers and sisters.
You are faithful and trustworthy;
May our words be seeds of goodness for the world:
Where there is shouting, let us practice listening;
Where there is confusion, let us inspire harmony;
Where there is ambiguity, let us bring clarity;
Where there is exclusion, let us offer solidarity;
Where there is sensationalism, let us use sobriety;
Where there is superficiality, let us raise real questions;
Where there is prejudice, let us awaken trust;
Where there is hostility, let us bring respect;
Where there is falsehood, let us bring truth. *Amen.*

-Pope Francis

Questions for reflection

Read back through Pope Francis' re-working of the Prayer of Saint Francis, and starting with the second line, think of a time when you believed something you read on social media and believed it without checking the facts.

What about a time when you judged someone harshly without trying to put yourself in their shoes?

Have you shouted when you should have listened? Excluded someone instead of including them?

Do you lean more toward being an instrument of God's peace or sowing dissension?

Thursday – Service

Saint Francis taught his fellow friars to use the greeting, "The Lord give you peace!"

"When you proclaim peace by your words," he said, "you must carry an even greater peace in your hearts. Let no one be provoked to anger by you, or be scandalized, but let your gentleness encourage all men to peace, good will, and mutual love. For our calling is to heal the wounded, to tend the maimed, and to bring home those who have lost their way. For many who today seem to us children of the Devil will yet become disciples of Christ."

Francis was mirroring what Jesus says in Matthew 5:21-26, "You have heard that it was said to those of ancient times, 'You shall not murder,' and 'whoever murders shall be liable to judgment.' But I say to you that if you are angry with a brother or sister, you will be liable to judgment, and if you insult a brother or sister, you will be liable to the council, and if you say, 'You fool,' you will be liable to the hell of fire. So when you are offering your gift at the altar, if you remember that your brother or sister has something against you, leave your gift there before the altar and go; first be reconciled to your brother or sister, and then come and offer your gift. Come to terms quickly with your accuser while you are on the way to court with him, or your accuser may hand you over to the judge and the judge to the guard, and you will be thrown into prison. Truly I tell you, you will never get out until you have paid the last penny."

Questions for reflection
Is there someone with whom you need to make peace? Imagine the faces of those with whom you might need reconciliation. Pray for Jesus to help you come to terms with making peace with this person or persons. Then, try and come up with a realistic plan for doing so. Reconciling with your enemies will bring you much peace.

Friday – Frank's Reflection

Victoria; our daughter, Griffin; and I were in Israel in 2000 to hike from the Mediterranean to the Sea of Galilee in a trip put together by the Community of the Holy Spirit, an order of Episcopal nuns. We were standing outside on a pleasant spring evening in Galilee as the blue dark sky dimmed toward night when warning sirens sounded an alarm. Everyone at the Kibbutz, where we were spending the night, continued as they were without pause. I asked someone what we were to do. "It's too late," he told me. "We can't make it to a shelter before the bombs land."

Recent attacks had all focused on nearby Kiriath Shimonah, of late, and it remained the presumed target when the sirens blared and loudspeakers directed us to a shelter. The rockets passed over us, and we could hear the distant rumble as the attack hit home right where everyone assumed it would land. And though the Kibbutzim had not been sure of this, they knew they were likely to be spared, and so they went about their lives. If this proved wrong, they would deal with a rocket attack and its aftermath.

Victoria and I returned to Israel on a study trip in Eastertide of 2018. We heard stories from an immigrant from the Bronx who became the spokesperson for Israel during the Second Intifada, when bomb attacks in the street or at weddings and other public events were common occurrences. We met Palestinian refugees in Bethlehem and learned of the desperation of a people wanting their historic homeland back as promised by the United Nations. We met so many people who shared their pains and sorrows, longing for others to understand their plight.

Generation after generation of pain and suffering is layered on the people who live where Jesus called on people to love their neighbors as themselves. The agape love that Jesus proclaimed means not seeking an eye for an eye, which seems too high a cost to pay after decades of killings. We came to see how distant the hope of peace is for the Holy Land.

The cost of unforgiveness is that peace eludes us in our lives and in our world, and so, we stack up more trauma on trauma. How many generations of Ukrainians will hold the unbearable sorrow of the war of this year? How many generations of children growing up in the crime-plagued neighborhoods of our country will find the camaraderie of a gang the only compelling alternative for community?

Jesus can bring true peace to the world, but only if we are ready to set aside the deep pain of generations of harm to offer forgiveness when crying out for vengeance is the natural human response. There have been hopeful exceptions, like the Truth and Reconciliation process in South Africa as Apartheid ended, but these are all too rare. But, as in that example, the answer cannot be imposed from the outside. Peace must come from within those in the conflict.

Questions for reflection
Do you have something you can't forgive?

What would it look like to let the hurt go?

Saturday – Worship

There are moments in life that suck all of the oxygen out of the air and take hope captive. If we are to speak of peace—that shalom that comes from God alone—we must speak of peace in the storm. For the students, staff, and their families of Marjorie Stoneman Douglas High School in Parkland, Florida, Ash Wednesday 2018 was a day of intense pain. Crosses inscribed in ashes made from the palms raised in Hosannas the previous year were still visible on the heads of some parents as they gathered in fear and confusion outside the school in the immediate aftermath of a shooting that left 17 people dead.

"For my family and many of the families affected, Lent this year was a visceral experience," Philip Schentrup, whose daughter Carmen was among those killed, said months later to a gathering at the General Convention of the Episcopal Church in Austin, Texas. He went on to describe that Lent as, "One of loss and lamentation. One of profound sorrow and helplessness."

Carmen had headed her youth group at St. Mary Magdalene Episcopal Church in Coral Springs, Florida, where she also sang in the choir. Her senseless death understandably brought the family to the edge of despair.

For Francis, God becoming human in Jesus was the decisive

act that made peace possible in the storms of life as we worship a God who has experienced storms in a boat on the Sea of Galilee as well as the metaphorical storms of life, including suffering and death. When we say that God will never leave or forsake us, we speak of that same God who in the person of Jesus knew real pain and is with us in the midst of sorrows that seem unbearable.

Philip Schentrup told the gathering in Austin how he had had a moment of inspired reflection after weeks of sorrow, "I understood at that moment that I had it all wrong. Carmen's murder and acts of much greater violence are not part of God's plan. God did not intend to inflict deep and lasting damage on my family."

He went on to say, "God is saddened by Carmen's murder and all the violence people are allowed to inflict on one another. God weeps for all his children." He went on to say, "God gave us free will–the ability to do good, to be complacent, to inflict harm. God gave us the prophets, his Son, and the Holy Spirit to show us the way. God wants us all to live into his path of love and kindness. God is waiting for us all to step up." For Philip and his family, stepping up is advocating for policies that can lessen the chance of massacres like the one that took their daughter.

There are so many storms of life during which we can't hold on to hope, and peace seems a distant memory. Victoria and I have both experienced this in times of tragedy in our lives, including when each of us lost a brother far too early. The path to peace is to stay in community, or to find your way back to community when you can. Gathering strength from others in worship is powerful, but so too is the still, small voice of God in prayer even when you don't have the strength to go to church. The sense of being held even in the abyss is real. While peace can seem far off in worship, it is in staying connected in prayer, even in prayers of lament said in hurt and anger, that we stay connected to the one who made us and loves us. In Jesus we can find that peace beyond understanding.

Questions for reflection
Have you been so hurt that you could not go to church? What brought you back?

When have you found peace in loss, even if well after the initial grief?

Christmas I

Love

Humility, simplicity, compassion, peace, love, creation, and joy are so interwoven in the life of Francis and the Franciscan way that they are difficult to untangle. And Franciscan spirituality, in general, is hard to encapsulate.

Franciscan John Quigley, summarizes Franciscan spirituality this way:

"It is not easy to put into a capsule the spirit and gifts of Franciscan thinking. Its hallmarks are simplicity, reverence, fraternity, ecumenism, ecology, interdependence, and dialogue. Its motto and salutation is 'Peace and All Good!'"

"Francis believed that God was nonviolent," he writes, "the God of Peace. This belief may be a simple presupposition for us today, but at the time when the Christian church was waging a Holy Crusade against its enemies, the Saracens, Francis' interpretation of the Gospel life and its demands was revolutionary. Francis saw it from the viewpoint of the poor, especially from the place of the poor, naked, suffering Christ. He had deep devotion to the God who is revealed as nonviolent and poor in the stable of Bethlehem, as abandoned on the cross, and as food in the Eucharist. God's meekness, humility, and poverty led Francis to… [identify] with the minores, the lower class within his society, and he passionately pointed to the Incarnation as the living proof of God's love. He frequently cried out in exasperation with the world, 'Love is not loved!'"

By its very nature, Love wants to be one with its beloved. That is how our salvation has been announced and realized by an Incarnate God. Jesus Christ's suffering and death confirms for us just how deeply committed God's love for his Creation was revealed in the Incarnation.

As Franciscan Friar Richard Rohr notes, "Everything, every scripture, every law, every action, history itself is to be interpreted in the light of the primacy of Love and Christ over all."

Advent, Christmas, and Epiphany with St. Francis

Sunday – A Franciscan Story

Once, when Saint Francis was traveling through the desert of Borgo San Sepolcro, he passed through a walled place called Monte Casale where he met a young and wealthy nobleman who told Francis he would like to be one of his friars.

When Francis seemed doubtful that, because of his wealth, the young man could take on the life of a poor friar, the youth protested that through the grace of Jesus Christ he could do anything. His answer pleased Francis so much that he immediately received him into the Order and gave him the name of Friar Angelo, making him guardian of the Hermitage at Monte Casale.

At that time, three notorious robbers were actively committing all manner of crime in that district. And one day, they arrived at the Hermitage and sought out Friar Angelo, demanding that he feed them.

Appalled that robbers would presume to devour the alms of food which had been sent to the friars there, he told them to leave and never show their faces in that place again. Furious, the robbers left in indignation.

Shortly after the robbers departed, Saint Francis arrived with a basket of bread and a small vessel of wine that he and his companion had begged. When Friar Angelo told Francis how he had driven the robbers away, the Saint rebuked him severely, saying that he had acted cruelly.

Sinners, Francis told him, are led back to God by gentleness. "For," he said, "our Master Jesus Christ, whose Gospel we have promised to observe, says that 'they that are whole need not a physician but they that are sick,' and that 'He was not come to call the righteous but sinners to repentance'; and therefore, He often did eat with them. Seeing, then, that you have acted contrary to the Holy Gospel of Christ, I command you, by holy obedience, that you immediately take this basket of bread and this vessel of wine and seek them diligently, through mountains and valleys, until you find them."

Once found, Francis told Friar Angelo that he must kneel before the robbers and confess to them his sin of cruelty, and to pray to them in the name of Francis to do evil no longer. If they do this, Francis said, he would provide for their needs.

So, while Angelo went in search of the robbers, Francis beseeched God to soften the hearts of the robbers so that they might be converted to repentance.

Angelo followed the orders of Saint Francis explicitly, and after he'd confessed and prayed with the robbers, their hearts were turned, agreeing to return with Angelo and begging forgiveness of Francis and God when they arrived.

Saint Francis received them "lovingly and benignly and consoled them with many examples, assuring them of the mercy of God." He explained to them how the mercy of God is infinite, and that even if their sins were infinite, the mercy of God is greater than anyone's sins. This is true according to the Gospel. As Saint Paul said, 'Christ the blessed came into this world to redeem sinners.'

Through the words of Francis, the three robbers renounced the devil and all his works, and the saint received them into the Order where they began to do great penance.

Questions for reflection
Has there ever been a time when you felt beyond the reach of God's love and mercy?

Has anyone ever treated you with love and kindness when you didn't feel you deserved it?

Monday – A Prayer

Most holy God, you sent the flame of your love to burn brightly among us as Immanuel, God with Us, in the person of Jesus. So enliven our love for you, our neighbors, and ourselves, that we might love not only those who love us, but also our enemies, and all whom you have made. Bring this self-giving love to its fullness in your coming reign where we will abide in this perfect love. *Amen.*

Tuesday – Victoria's Reflection

As Tina Turner so famously sang, "What's love got to do with it?" Well, according to Saint Francis, and, of course, Jesus, everything.

It's difficult to speak about love in a language in which saying, "I love this chocolate" or "I love you" to your spouse hold two completely different meanings. English speakers say "I love" so much that it has almost become meaningless.

Not all languages are as deficient as English. As Robert Johnson notes in his book, *The Fisher King and the Handless Maiden*:

"Sanskrit has 96 words for love; ancient Persian has 80,

Greek three, and English only one. This is indicative of the poverty of awareness or emphasis that we give to that tremendously important realm of feeling. Eskimos have 30 words for snow, because it is a life-and-death matter to them to have exact information about the element they live with so intimately. If we had a vocabulary of 30 words for love... we would immediately be richer and more intelligent in this human element so close to our heart. An Eskimo probably would die of clumsiness if he had only one word for snow; we are close to dying of loneliness because we have only one word for love. Of all the Western languages, English may be the most lacking when it comes to feeling."

And perhaps that is the problem. Perhaps English is deficient because we think of love as a feeling and not as what Christ truly meant by love–an action. Feelings are untrustworthy. Love is an act of the will.

Former Presiding Bishop John Allin said, "It is easier to act yourself into a new way of thinking, than to think yourself into a new way of acting." He didn't say, "feel your way." Love is a choice, a verb.

As Joni Woolf—a parishioner at Calvary, Americus, who assisted in editing these devotions—told us, "Act out what you know to be good. Perhaps it will feel good. It may not. The point is 'to do justly, love mercy, and walk humbly with God (Micah 6:8).'"

Paul defines real love in 1 Corinthians 13:4-8. And if you look at what he says in terms of action rather than feeling it makes more sense:

"Love is patient; love is kind; love is not envious or boastful or arrogant or rude. It does not insist on its own way; it is not irritable; it keeps no record of wrongs; it does not rejoice in wrongdoing but rejoices in the truth. It bears all things, believes all things, hopes all things, endures all things. Love never ends."

Clearly, love is not easy. It is an ongoing journey, growing in love as we grow in Christ; giving of ourselves as we remember that love is measured by sacrifice. The sacrifice might be as small as a smile on a day when we feel down ourselves or not saying an unkind word when we are feeling grouchy. On the opposite end of the spectrum, sometimes love can mean sacrificing one's life. Regardless, as Day 25 of the Franciscan Principles notes: "Love is the distinguishing feature of all true disciples of Christ who wish to dedicate themselves to him as his servants."

Advent, Christmas, and Epiphany with St. Francis

Wednesday – Quotations

We thank you
That through your Son you created us,
And that through the holy love you had for us
You brought about his birth
As true God and true man
By the glorious, ever virgin, most blessed, holy Mary…
-Rule of 1221, Chapter XXIII

Question for reflection
Knowing that God has True Love for all God's Creation and loves everything and everyone equally, how close have you come to experiencing real love?

Thursday – Service

In this series of meditations inspired by the life of a superhero of the faith we find in Jesus, it would be too easy to have Grace turn to Law, inspiring us to do more and more. Yet within Jesus' distillation of the Law and the Prophets, we find two words ttoo often ignored: "as yourself." Jesus did not just tell us to love God with all our heart, mind, soul, and strength, and to love our neighbors. He said we are to love our neighbors as ourselves. This corrective matters as we do not show our love of God by abusing ourselves. We do not best serve others by so immersing ourselves in that service that we lose sight of that command to love our neighbors as ourselves.

When it comes to the ways we serve God, true discernment includes not just deciding what to do, but also in deciding what to stop. We all go through seasons of life, and in those varied seasons, we often have little time to set something down in order to focus on how God is showing up. For the new parents, time with the baby and toddler is so all-encompassing that there is little room for much else, and for those with other toddlers in the house, a newborn is all the more a gift that demands time and attention. The same is true when we find ourselves caring for an aging parent. Then there is the compassion fatigue that can hinder our ability to serve as we first did in some ministry from which we need a time of rest.

The main way to do this is setting down some commitment. Love can mean saying no to an opportunity. When we continually do more and more, we are putting trust in our own abilities rather than truly trusting God. The needs of the world are more than any of us can meet. Setting limits is a way of honoring God as much as serving honors God.

Questions for reflection
When have you experienced a season of life in which you needed to set aside some of your previous priorities?

What do you need to stop doing now?

Advent, Christmas, and Epiphany with St. Francis

Capoeira in a street in Poca Olho as described in Frank's reflection.

Friday – Frank's Reflection

"Whoever gives even a cup of cold water…"

I thought of Jesus' saying as I looked at the tin cup of clear, cold water, held out by a boy beaming at me. The sun was beating down. I was covered in sweat. Yet, my first thought was of the signs posted all over the neighborhood warning of the danger in drinking the water without boiling it first. I was in the most dangerous part of the big and growing Brazilian metropolis of Belo Horizonte, a city of two million people.

This was 1994 and I was still a few years from starting seminary. I went to Brazil with Jean-Paul, a friend who had been an exchange student when we were together at Georgia Southern. He was making a documentary film on the martial art dance called Capoeira. Capoeira is a uniquely Brazilian blend of gymnastics, dance, music, and fighting.

We were specifically documenting the work of a group of Capoeira teachers who gave free lessons in a deadly slum. In Brazil, you take Capoeira lessons the way one might learn Tae Kwon Do here. To take part, you had to stay away from drugs—whether running drugs for dealers or taking them—and to stay in school. Raimundo, who started the program, and his fellow teachers emphasized the communal aspect of Capoeira to build up a community of hope. They gave respect in a place that taught kids they were worthless. The self-giving service I saw in Capoeira teachers in their 20s and 30s—going back week after week for years to lift up kids who would otherwise be lost and left out—was not a Christian program and yet I saw the agape love of God run through it.

The day before I left Brazil, Raimundo and I rode into Poca Olho on his motorcycle. We found boys from the program playing in the street. Raimundo worked with them on their moves. Then it was my turn. The kids laughed at my awkward attempts at Capoeira. Soon we were playing with abandon in the sweltering heat. When we stopped to catch our breath, a boy I had just been fighting ran off and came back quickly with a tin cup of cold water. I knew he offered it in love, and I could not turn him down.

I never did get sick. Now, when I remember this, I recall that boy grinning from ear to ear as he offered me a tin cup of cool water. This is the world as God sees it. The roles were all reversed. I was the American who had flown down to Brazil with my expensive photography equipment. He was the kid in the slum with seemingly nothing to offer. And yet, it was he who was reaching out to me. He was the host, and I was the guest right there in the street. As our Presiding Bishop, Michael Curry, likes to say, something like that just smells like Jesus. It's got Jesus all over it. This is what self-giving love looks like.

Questions for reflection
When have you experienced an unexpected offering out of love?

Saturday – Worship

As Francis saw Christmas as the Feast of Feasts, he dreamed of a way to make the otherwise inexpressible love of God real for those who gathered to worship. The setting would be the most important part of the liturgy. Having worshiped in Bethlehem years earlier, Francis knew of a cave near Greccio that he could use to recreate Jesus' birth. He asked John, a layman he knew well, to make a manger, fill it with straw, and bring a donkey and an ox, to graze near the altar John was to build over the manger in the cave.

By that winter of 1223, Francis was already famed for his pure, simple devotion to Jesus. When Francis called others to join him for Christmas Eucharist in a cave, the crowd was immense. The cave would reveal the humble birth of our savior. Not only was this Mass to be celebrated in a cave, but a live ox and donkey can't make it through the lead up to the liturgy without gracing the hay with offerings of their own. This was for Francis the ineffable part of the Incarnation. God became human. And in so doing entered into the messiness of human existence. Francis wanted worshippers to experience how God is present in the reality of their daily lives.

Thomas of Celano, who was living closely with Francis, described the liturgy. In beautiful vestments, the Deacon, Francis, chanted the holy Gospel with, "an earnest, sweet, clear and loud-sounding voice; inviting all to the highest rewards….Then he preached to the people who stood around, and uttered mellifluous words concerning the birth of the poor King and the little town of Bethlehem."

This was the first live Nativity, a reminder of divine simplicity for a church worshiping in Latin, which the common people did not understand, and in cathedrals where the rich and powerful had the places of honor.

Advent, Christmas, and Epiphany with St. Francis

Francis moved the pomp associated with the liturgies of the church to a place that revealed what was always true: God sides with the poor, the humble, the outcast.

Francis saw the deeper magic of the Nativity: the Holy Trinity could have stood back as righteous judge rather than living among us. But God's love for us was so great, that God always planned to live among us in the person of Jesus, and thereby entered fully into what it means to be human. This is why Francis invited worshippers to join him in worshiping God in the reality of their daily lives, messy as they may be.

Jesus is Immanuel, God with us, just as Francis illustrated in a powerful way to those who walked by torchlight to a cave outside Greccio. Knowing ourselves to be both fully known and fully loved by the God who loved us before he made us changes everything.

Francis preaching to birds by an unknown illustrator.

Christmas II

Creation

His ability to see the footprints of God inscribed on everything in Creation allowed Saint Francis to find God wherever he went in the world. And finding God in the things of creation led Francis into the loving arms of Jesus, for Christ is the Word of God made visible in the world.

"Francis came to realize that it is Christ who sanctifies creation and transforms it into the sacrament of God," writes Franciscan author Ilia Delio. "The intimate link between creation and Incarnation revealed to Francis that the whole of creation is the place to encounter God. As his eyes opened to the holiness of creation, he came to see that there is nothing trivial or worthless. Rather, all created things point beyond themselves to their Creator."

Saint Bonaventure, a First Order Friar and scholar who died in 1274, describes the contemplative vision of Francis as contuition, or, seeing things for what they truly are in God. In his book, *The Life of Saint Francis of Assisi*, Bonaventure writes:

"In beautiful things he contuited Beauty itself and through the footprints impressed in things he followed his Beloved everywhere, out of them all making for himself a ladder through which he could climb up to lay hold of him who is utterly desirable. . . . He savored in each and every creature—as in so many rivulets—that fontal Goodness, and . . . sweetly encouraged them to praise the Lord."

Francisan author and speaker Richard Rohr sums it up well, "Francis had a unique ability to call others—animals, plants, and elements—'brother' and 'sister' because he himself was a little brother. He granted other beings and things mutuality, subjectivity, 'personhood,' and dignity because he first honored his own dignity as a son of God. The world of things was a transparent two-way mirror for him, which some of us would call a fully 'sacramental' universe."

Advent, Christmas, and Epiphany with St. Francis

Sunday – A Franciscan Story

A story told by Ugolino di Monte Santa Maria in *The Little Flowers of Saint Francis of Assisi* is one of the many that abound to show his unique connection to creation. It relates how Francis, while on his way between Cannaio and Bevagno, looked up to see an infinite number of birds perched in the trees alongside the road.

"You shall await me here," Francis said, stopping and speaking to his companions, "and I will go and preach to the birds, my sisters." Francis then left the road and walked into a field where a number of birds were gathered on the ground.

As he began to preach to them, the birds in the trees fluttered to the ground, and along with the others, stood still until Francis had finished preaching. They refused to depart until the saint gave them his blessing, and according to Friar Masseo, as Francis passed through them, his mantle brushing their feathers, they still did not move.

According to Ugolino, this is what Francis preached to the birds:

"My sisters the birds, you are much obliged to God your creator, and always and in every place you ought to praise Him, because He has given you liberty to fly wherever you will and has clothed you with twofold and threefold raiment. Moreover, He preserved your seed in Noah's Ark that your race might not be destroyed. Again, you are obliged to Him for the element of the air which He has appointed for you. Furthermore, you sow not neither do you reap, yet God feeds you and gives you rivers and fountains from which to drink. He gives you mountains and valleys for your refuge, and high trees in which to build your nests. And, since you know neither how to sew or spin, God clothes you and your little ones; so, clearly, your Creator loves you, seeing that He gives you so many benefits. Guard yourselves, therefore, you sisters the birds, from the sin of ingratitude and be ever mindful to give praise to God."

As Francis was speaking these words to them, the birds began to open their beaks and wings, stretch out their necks, and bow their heads toward the ground. They showed by their movement and their song that Francis had given them much happiness.

When he had finished preaching, Saint Francis made the sign of the Cross over them and allowed that they might now depart. The birds rose into the air, singing, and separated themselves into four bands flying, flying east, west, south, and north in the shape of a cross.

Questions for reflection
This is just one of the many, many stories about the

saint's close connection to God's Creation. What is your relationship with Creation?

How do you show the reverence or respect you have for the outdoors and all the creatures it holds?

Monday – A Prayer

Creator God, you spoke and the cosmos came into being, the seas and the dry land, plants bearing seed, and all the animals on the face of the earth. You made humankind in your image and likeness and gave us dominion over all the earth that we might care for all that you made. In our selfishness and greed, humans have spoiled all that you had made and called very good. Assist us, we pray, to find joy in the world that you have formed as we join with others in serving you by fostering the healing you long for in all creation. This we ask for the sake of him through whom all things were made, your Son Jesus Christ our Lord. *Amen.*

Tuesday – Victoria's Reflection

My life has been so intrinsically tied to Creation since I was young that it is difficult to pick out just one example that was particularly meaningful to me. From exploring Walden Pond and Acadia National Park when I was very young to spending days on the lakes, rivers, and reservoirs of California in our houseboat, The Golden Goose, to spending six months backpacking from Georgia to Maine, my life abounds with examples of time spent outdoors.

Even when I can't be outside, I have always enjoyed having my home office (never always possible in any of my numerous workplaces over the years) near a window. For the past eight years, I have been able to look out my window and watch the numerous birds and squirrels, butterflies and lizards, enjoy the flowers, birdfeeders, and birdbath in our backyard. I even once watched a raccoon picking through the fallen seed.

In the foreword to artist Courtney Milne's classic work *The Sacred Earth*, the Dalai Lama reminds us that Mother Earth not only provides us with breath, water, food, clothing and shelter, "but she even serves as a source of inspiration. Throughout history people all over the world have identified particular places as sacred."

Groves of trees, mountains, rivers, islands, and more have been marked as holy ground since the beginning of time, and are often sites of pilgrimage for many people.

But sacredness is everywhere, even in our backyards, and it varies every day and with every season. As Courtney Milne notes, "as long as one observes deeply."

Milne's vision as an artist was "to reveal life's unfolding mystery—not to try to solve it." And that mystery can be discovered in one's own backyard or front yard, or in your local park, or a walk through the forest, or alongside a river.

As Franciscan sister Ilia Delio explains, "Francis came to realize that it is Christ who sanctifies creation and transforms it into the sacrament of God. The intimate link between creation and Incarnation revealed to Francis that the whole of creation is the place to encounter God. As his eyes opened to the holiness of creation, he came to see that there is nothing trivial or worthless. Rather, all created things point beyond themselves to their Creator."

Even if it's just for a few minutes daily, one can always find a reason to revel in God's creation whether it be early morning sunlight bathing a flower in its rosy light or the rapidly wagging tail of your beloved dog. There are myriad ways to acknowledge that God's Creation is a daily and important part of our lives.

Wednesday – Quotation

Canticle of the Creatures

Most High, all-powerful, good Lord,
Yours are the praises, the glory, and the honor,
   and all blessing.
To You alone, Most High, do they belong, and no human
   is worthy to mention Your name.

Praised be You, my Lord, with all Your creatures,
   especially Sir Brother Sun,
Who is the day and through whom You give us light.

And he is beautiful and radiant with great splendor;
   and bears a likeness of You, Most High One.

Praised be You, my Lord, through Sister Moon and
   the stars, in heaven You formed them clear and precious
   and beautiful.

Praised be You, my Lord, through Brother Wind, and
   through the air, cloudy and serene, and every
   kind of weather, through whom You give sustenance
   to Your creatures.

Praised be You, my Lord, through Sister Water, who is
   very useful and humble and precious and chaste.

Advent, Christmas, and Epiphany with St. Francis

Praised be You, my Lord, through Brother Fire, through whom You light the night, and he is beautiful and playful and robust and strong.

Praised be You, my Lord, through our Sister Mother Earth, who sustains and governs us, and who produces various fruit with colored flowers and herbs.

Praised be You, my Lord, through those who give pardon for Your love, and bear infirmity and tribulation.

Blessed are those who endure in peace for by You, Most High, shall they be crowned.

Praised be You, my Lord, through our Sister Bodily Death, from whom no one living can escape.

Woe to those who die in mortal sin.

Blessed are those whom death will find in Your most holy will, for the second death shall do them no harm.

Praise and bless my Lord and give Him thanks and serve Him with great humility.

-Saint Francis of Assisi

Francis reveled in Creation, even going so far as rescuing worms from being trodden upon on dry and dusty roads to returning caught fish to their watery homes. He even welcomed death as part of the natural order of life.

Questions for reflection
Where are you when it comes to respecting God's Creation? When you use water, for example, do you consider all that it has taken for it to pour so freely from your faucet, or do you take it for granted?

How about insects and other small creatures? If they are in your home, do you trap them and set them free? Do you exterminate some and not others?

Finally, how do you feel about your own mortality? Have you prepared for it by setting your preferences for your burial service or do you avoid talking about it at all?

Thursday – Service

Statues of Saint Francis, often featuring birdbaths, abound. Many churches, even those not named for the saint, have a Francis statue tucked away somewhere. But, Francis reminds us that nature consists not only of animals and plants, but of ourselves—our bodies and souls. Nature, itself, is catholic, as it includes all that is. From deserts to snow-covered wastelands, all is holy. And to God, it is all beautiful, a work of art.

"Look at the birds of the air," Jesus tells us, "they neither sow nor reap nor gather into barns, and yet your heavenly Father feeds them. Are you not of more value than they? And which of you by worrying can add a single hour to your span of life? And why do you worry about clothing? Consider the lilies of the field, how they grow; they neither toil nor spin, yet I tell you, even Solomon in all his glory was not clothed like one of these. But if God so clothes the grass of the field, which is alive today and tomorrow is thrown into the oven, will he not much more clothe you—you of little faith? Therefore do not worry, saying, 'What will we eat?' or 'What will we drink?' or 'What will we wear?' For it is the gentiles who seek all these things, and indeed your heavenly Father knows that you need all these things. But seek first the kingdom of God and his righteousness, and all these things will be given to you as well. So do not worry about tomorrow, for tomorrow will bring worries of its own. Today's trouble is enough for today." (Matthew 6:26-34)

Questions for reflection

Recall two ways in which you have cared for Mother Earth over the last two days. Now, think of two ways in which you could show Creation respect for all it gives you.

When was the last time you enjoyed a sunrise or sunset? Is there a way in which you could learn to love nature more? Do your patterns of consumption show that you respect the Earth and its creatures, or do they show an abuse of Creation?

Friday – Frank's Reflection

An unexpectedly prophetic encounter with a biology professor led to me reframing how I see our stewardship of creation. He was retiring from a career teaching at Shorter College, a Baptist-affiliated school in Rome, Georgia, where I worked at the time as a photographer for the local newspaper. I was sent to take pictures of the professor at his home. His yard boasted an enviable vegetable garden and chicken coops that provided sustenance as he sought to stay close to our sources of food.

As I took pictures, I asked him what he had learned from decades of teaching life sciences. He said that he had come to hope for a cataclysm that would only kill hundreds of millions of people or perhaps even a billion or two of us. I was stunned. What was he talking about? His hope was for mass deaths?

He went on to explain that humans were blind to how our actions were having a catastrophic global impact. The path we are on is unsustainable, he told me. We could not even provide the basics we counted on in Georgia for everyone around the world. There were no energy solutions that would have everyone in air-conditioned comfort eating foods with no thought to the seasons. The professor was sure that it would take something epic to make likely that large scale change in human behavior needed to save humankind.

He had no fears for the planet. Earth would and could easily continue, healing itself over centuries if humans were to die off. His concern was not for the Earth *per se*, but for whether we would endure as a species.

This was the mid 1980s. I had yet to binge on dystopian novels and movies. It was the first time I heard someone offering such a stark view of the future. The oddest thing was that his hope was for the Earth, itself, to get our attention before it was too late for us.

A decade later, I studied Hebrew with Dr. Ellen Davis who showed me the close connection between humankind and the Earth. Genesis calls the first human, Adam. In that same passage, the Hebrew word for the fertile soil is used: *Adamah*. We are, she taught us, "humans of the humus." We were made to live close to the soil, the dust into which God breathed a soul. God made everything and called it good and then told Adam and Eve to steward creation.

On the day I photographed the professor, I did not focus on the garden and the chicken coop as integral to the story he was telling me of our unsustainable way of living. I would later read Wendall Berry, the farmer and poet who also speaks prophetically about the cost of turning away from agrarian values out of hubristic greed. I then came to see how the professor's micro-scale farm was the point. The connection to creation he felt in working the soil and tending the chickens were integral to his view of how humanity needed a wake-up call and to his hope that those who survived would listen.

Questions for reflection
When have you experienced a closeness to creation?

How might you foster a closer connection to your sources of food?

Saturday – Worship

If God created everything then it would follow that everything involved with worship is part of God's creation. But there is one major exception that I have seen in more than one church: artificial flowers. Plants in church, especially the altar flowers, are there to represent resurrection and life. If they are made of plastic or silk or some other thing other than a living plant, then you might as well have nothing at all. Seriously. If your church cannot afford to have living flowers on the altar every week then invest in a house plant of some sort. And if plain green seems too boring, then find something variegated.

Having flowers and living plants in your church space is

not the only way to bring a focus on God's creation into your church. Another way is prayer. Using Prayer C for the Eucharist is one obvious way, but another way is what has become known as eco-prayer. And the best thing? Eco-prayer is something an individual can do. It's simple:

1) Choose: A People, A Place, A Plant, or An Animal that you LOVE.
2) Commit: To Praying for them and the entire Eco-System that they live in every day with positive intention.

For example, if you care for wolves, pray for them to thrive (or visualize them as healthy) and for the mountains and forests that they live in. You can also include a prayer for the people who live in and influence their ecosystem as well.

To help with this, you could find a picture of the thing that you have chosen and put it where you will see it every day to remind you to pray (on the bathroom mirror, car dash, the refrigerator, over your desk, wherever makes sense).

Finally, you can take part in your diocese's Creation Care Commission. Can you think of any other ways to bring reverence for God's Creation into your worship?

The Adoration of the Magi by Bartolo di Fredi (c. 1390)

Epiphany

Joy

The only thing Saint Francis was interested in achieving was to live his life in as close an imitation of Jesus as possible. And he was able to do this with a "perfect joy" that came from letting go of his ego.

Theologian Adolf Holl noted that Francis was born just as people began to measure time by clocks instead of by church bells. So, Francis stopped counting when the Church started counting. Instead of continuing the church system that used merit (buying indulgences, etc.), Francis moved to a different system—the immeasurable economy of God's grace. God gives fully and without reserve.

As the world settled into a downward spiral of production and consumption that would lead to a pillaged and plundered Earth, Francis decided instead to love Mother Earth. He chose to live simply and barefoot upon her, cherishing God's creation, and finding joy in everything.

Francis, and Clare, fell in love with both the humanity and the humility of Jesus. They felt that Jesus was someone to imitate and not just to worship as the Son of God. Francis put his emphasis on action, practice, and lifestyle, which was revolutionary for the time and remains so to this day.

Questions for reflection
What is an action, practice or something in your lifestyle that brings you joy on a daily basis?

Sunday – A Franciscan Story

Francis aspired to an experience of joy that was tied to being faithful to God rather than delight in one's circumstances. Saint Francis dictated the meaning of true joy to a fellow monk:

"What true joy is: A messenger comes and says…that my brothers have gone to all the unbelievers and converted all of them to the faith; again, that I have so much grace from God that I heal the sick and perform many miracles: I tell you that joy does not consist in any of these things.

"What then is true joy? I return to Perugia and arrive there in the dead of night; and it is winter time, muddy and so cold that icicles have formed on the edges of my habit and keep striking my legs, and blood flows from such wounds. And all covered with mud and cold, I come to the gate and after I have knocked and called for some time, a brother comes and asks, 'Who are you?' I answer, 'Brother Francis.' "And he says, 'go away; this is not the proper hour for going about; you may not come in.' And when I insist, he answers, 'Go away, you are a simple and stupid person; we are so many and we have no need of you. You are certainly not coming to us at this hour!' And I stand again at the door and say: 'For the love of God, take me in tonight.'

"And he answers, 'I will not. Go to the Crossiers' place and ask there.' I tell you this: If I had the patience and did not become upset, there would be true joy in this and true virtue and the salvation of the soul.'"

Question for reflection
Francis wanted to conform his life to God's will in such a way that even cruelty of a fellow brother of the religious order he founded could not take away his joy. He felt that if he could find patience even in the midst of suffering, he would find the key to finding joy in all things. Have you found joy beyond the circumstances of life or is your delight always tied to things going your way?

Monday – A Prayer

Life-giving God, fill us with that inexpressible and glorious joy that is found in you, that with Blessed Francis, we may find that delight in you even in the midst of a fallen world. As we put our trust in you more and more may we overflow with that hope of the Spirit that others may see and feel our joy and so be drawn to your son, our Savior, Jesus. This we ask in the Name of the one who came that we might have life, and have it abundantly, who with you and the Holy Spirit lives and reigns now and forever. *Amen.*

Tuesday – Victoria's Reflection

There are nearly 270 references to joy in the Bible, many of which are in the psalms. And, of course, we cannot forget that joy is a Fruit of the Spirit named in Galatians 5:22-23: "the fruit of the Spirit is love, joy, peace, patience, kindness, generosity, faithfulness, gentleness, and self-control."

And yet it is a very human condition to think of joy as something that brings one an overwhelming sense of happiness like gazing at the face of a newborn child or grandchild. But, as with most everything, joy is best consumed in moderation. Mountaintop experiences are amazing and should not be forgotten, but in the quotidian, joy should be found in the simple things—that first sip of coffee or tea in the morning, a Scripture reading that seems to speak directly to one's current situation, the scent of a flower, a cardinal splashing merrily in a birdbath, singing along to a favorite hymn in church. The list goes on and on and varies from person to person.

Day Twenty Eight – The Third Note: Joy in the Principles of TSSF says:

"Tertiaries, rejoicing in the Lord always, show in our lives the grace and beauty of divine joy. We remember that we follow the Son of Man, who came eating and drinking, who loved the birds and the flowers, who blessed little children, who was a friend of tax collectors and sinners, and who sat at the tables of both the rich and the poor. We delight in fun and laughter, rejoicing in God's world, its beauty, and its living creatures, calling nothing common or unclean. We mix freely with all people, ready to bind up the broken-hearted and to bring joy into the lives of others."

And that is why every day, no matter how I feel (tired, grumpy, down, happy, blessed, you-name-it), I try to find something of note to bring me joy. Sometimes it can be as simple as one of my cats wanting some attention or wishing my daughter luck on an exam or presentation. Sometimes it is enjoying the bounty of the beautiful vegetables and fruit in my weekly Farm Bag or the satisfaction of finishing a project.

Joy can be found in so many places and in so many things. Some people have the practice of writing down one thing they are thankful for each day. I would add to that. In addition to something one is thankful for, also note something that has brought joy that day.

Wednesday – Quotations

"The devil is most happy when he can snatch from a servant of God true joy of spirit. He carries dust with him to throw into the smallest chinks of conscience and thus soil one's mental candor and purity of life. But if joy of spirit fills the heart, the serpent shoots his deadly venom in vain."

–*Saint Francis in Thomas of Celano's,* Second Life of Saint Francis

Questions for reflection
How easy is it for your joy to be snatched away? When faced with adversity, do you shy away from it? Sink into depression? Worry and lament until you are ill? Flounder in the stress and anxiety it causes? Or can you face adversity as a challenge, rising to the occasion, confident that with God's help you can see it through?

Thursday – Service

Francis took the concept of joy to the extreme, even rebuking one of his friars for his sad and gloomy countenance as they were walking along a road. He told the friar to keep his sorrow between himself and God and to pray for the healing that would bring joy.

"But in front of me and others show yourself as always having joy," Francis told him. "For it is not fitting for a servant of God to show sadness outwardly, or to have a clouded face."

Strong words, but fortunately we know so much more today. Was the friar just feeling down at the moment or was he actually depressed? Perhaps he could have used someone to speak to honestly about his pain or even an antidepressant.

Regardless, it is not a bad idea to remind ourselves daily that God's unconditional love for us is something that should be a cause for joy and that nothing, not even a bad day, will separate us from the love of God.

Joy should not be confused with happiness, which can come and go, and that is why it is so important to find the joy in little things.

After Gabriel announced to Mary that she would be the mother of the Messiah, she went to see her cousin Elizabeth to share her joy. Also miraculously pregnant, Elizabeth felt the child within her womb leap with joy. When was the last time you leapt with joy (if not literally, figuratively)?

Think back over the past few months to the times when you felt joyful. Was the joy caused by something that was brought about by another person? If so, write a letter/email/text to the person who brought you joy, thanking them for having brought a moment of joy into your life.

Friday – Frank's Reflection

Joy is, in my experience, the sneakiest Fruit of the Spirit. Joy is a breath-taking gift from God when a moment proves to be more full of meaning than seems possible. One of the most wonderful surprises in being the Bishop of Georgia has been the many occasions that have sparked deep joy. But to explain what I mean, I will have to let you in on what this vocation is really like from the inside.

Picture me in the museum-quality cope and mitre given by the Archbishop of the Anglican Church in Japan to Bishop Albert Rhett Stuart in the 1950s. I would like to tell you I feel holy. Instead, I find myself slipping into imposter syndrome again, sure that I do not have what I need for this call.

At a practical level, I am trying to not get in my head, simply stay focused on the words of the liturgy, meaning the words as I pray them. I look at the name tag and say the name of the confirmand, assisting her in kneeling, and pray, "Strengthen, O Lord, your servant Susan with your Holy Spirit; empower her for your service; and sustain her all the days of her life." Being fully present with the person I am praying for in the moment has to be, and surely is, enough.

One afternoon, I felt that creeping sense of not being enough as I drove to an in-home confirmation for a homebound parishioner in Hospice care. She sat on the couch next to her husband with 20 friends gathered in their living and dining rooms. "All the days of her life" seems too short a time-period. Yet I was given the grace to see that this prayer is not for this life alone as her life in Christ will continue beyond the grave. The joy of that moment is beyond words.

At my first in-person convention as bishop, the day was cold, windy, and rainy with news reports saying the flooding was near hurricane levels. More than 200 people arrived damp and cold for the Convention Eucharist in a tent in the field at Honey Creek. With everyone in, we dropped the sides, cutting back the wind, and the tent warmed and Jesus showed up. Then we enjoyed some good Southern cooking with fried chicken, collard greens, and macaroni and cheese.

Feast of Feasts

Worship in a tent at Honey Creek for the Diocesan Convention.

A DJ provided music, and we danced as the rain continued. Watching the people of the Diocese delighted to be with each other was life giving. Then the Rev. David Wantland and I ended up taking over the dance floor as all gathered around watching us dance to Abba's "Dancing Queen." I am not a dancer by any stretch, but I could follow as he led, spinning me across the floor. What a surprisingly joyful moment.

I am at peace with not having what this call needs as that keeps me dependent on God. When I think I can rely on my own gifts, I fall flat. But when I can get out of my head and let the Spirit do as the Spirit will, I find myself surprised by the joy in those moments of grace.

Question for reflection
When have you been surprised by joy?

Saturday – Worship

It almost seems like a no-brainer to write about "joy" as an aspect of worship. After all, if attending church didn't bring us some comfort, happiness, connection, joy, we probably wouldn't go at all. Or, at least, we might find some excuse not to be there as often as we might if we had friends or family that would question our absence.

But I think it is possible to become so accustomed to the order of service that you might miss things that once brought you joy. So, I am going to suggest an experiment. The next time you attend church, pay attention to every aspect of the service.

Before the service, look at your surroundings. Is there some aspect of your church's architecture that brings you joy? What about the windows, whether stained glass or clear? Just take a look around and reflect on why you return to this space.

Watch the Processional carefully. Is there someone (a choir member, an acolyte, a lay minister, the priest, deacon) that seems to be truly enjoying their role?

Listen to the hymns. Is there one that you particularly enjoy singing?

Focus on the readings. Is there a line or word that has particular meaning for you?

During the Peace, look around to see who is enjoying the connection with other worshippers and who is alone.

When you partake of the Eucharist, participate completely.

Try to make a habit of finding joy in worship every week so that if you have a difficult day in the week that follows, you can reflect back on how you felt on Sunday.

Afterward

We trust that this seven weeks from Advent through the week after the Epiphany has introduced you to Franciscan spirituality in a way that reveals it is to be nothing more than simply following Jesus. Francis' example of a Christ-like life transformed the Italy of his youth within his own lifetime. By the time of his death, Francis could see many thousands of lives transformed by his call for repentance and simplicity of life.

Francis took his mustard seed of faith and used it to trust, that despite his fear, he could hug a leper. In conquering his fear, he found the faith to work among lepers. And so, again and again, his steps of faith emboldened Francis to trust God more. It is the same for us. Each step of faith strengthens our trust in God. Then we are enabled to follow Jesus even more boldly.

None of the life of faith is about serving God in order to earn God's love. God loves us freely, wholeheartedly,

Feast of Feasts

undeservedly. In humility in the care of creation as in all the ways we might serve God by serving others, we are only responding to God's love in loving others as God loves us.

> "Let your religion be less of a theory
> and more of a love affair."
>
> *-G.K. Chesterton*

*Madonna and Child with Saints Francis and Clare
by Cima da Conegliano (c. 1510)*

www.ingramcontent.com/pod-product-compliance
Lightning Source LLC
Chambersburg PA
CBHW070434010526
44118CB00014B/2042